Hari Walner's
Continuous-Line
QUILTING DESIGNS

80 Patterns for Blocks, Borders, Corners & Backgrounds

C&T PUBLISHING

Text and Artwork copyright © 2010 by Hari Walner

Artwork copyright © 2010 by C&T Publishing, Inc.

Publisher: Amy Marson

Creative Director: Gailen Runge

Acquisitions Editor: Susanne Woods

Editor: Lynn Koolish

Technical Editor: Mary E. Flynn

Copyeditor/Proofreader: Wordfirm Inc.

Cover Designer: Kristen Yenche

Book Designer: Rose Wright

Page Layout Artist: Casey Dukes

Production Coordinator: Zinnia Heinzmann

Production Editor: Alice Mace Nakanishi

Illustrator: Hari Walner

Photography by Christina Carty-Francis and Diane Pedersen of C&T Publishing, Inc., unless otherwise noted; photography by Dennis Dolan on pages 67, 102, and 103.

Published by C&T Publishing, Inc., P.O. Box 1456, Lafayette, CA 94549

Library of Congress Cataloging-in-Publication Data

Walner, Hari, 1940-

Hari Walner's continuous-line quilting designs : 80 patterns for blocks, borders, corners & backgrounds / Hari Walner.

    p. cm.

Includes index.

ISBN 978-1-60705-176-3 (softcover)

1. Machine quilting. 2. Quilting--Patterns. 3. Quilting--Design. I. Title. II. Title: Continuous-line quilting designs.

TT835.W35635 2010

746.46--dc22

                    2010019011

Printed in China

10 9 8 7 6 5 4 3 2

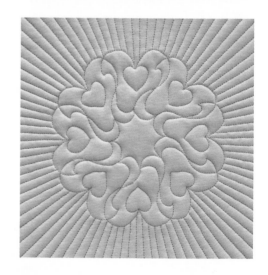

Contents

Acknowledgments

A Special Note …

Diana McClun and Linda V. Taylor are two outstanding teachers who continue to spread the good word of quilting through their belief in, and support of, their students and other teachers. They have constantly demonstrated their deep commitment to our beautiful art form.

Diana introduces students to beginning quiltmaking techniques on the sewing machine in such an understandable, encouraging, and gentle way that new quilters have no choice but to be excited about continuing the adventure. Diana has co-authored several books and is one of the founders of the Empty Spools Seminars in Pacific Grove, California.

Linda took the lead and showed by example that longarm machines are indeed legitimate quilting tools. She then developed heirloom techniques and designs for the longarm machine that she unselfishly shares with legions of students. Linda has taught through her television shows, DVDs, conference appearances, international workshops, and in her studio.

My personal gratitude to these women is for the over-the-top confidence and encouragement they have both shown in my quilting ideas and teaching skills. I am deeply appreciative. Our quilt world is greatly enriched by their generous spirits.

It takes a village to write a book. Thank you …

… to Gordon Snow, my partner in every way, for his consistent encouragement and belief in my ideas and abilities, and for all those nights of take-out or macaroni and cheese dinners.

… to Ivena Roush, my friend and quilting neighbor, for generously giving of her time and her enthusiastic attitude in proofreading and making helpful suggestions early in this bookmaking process.

… to C&T Publishing, for the interest in wanting me to do this third book. The C&T staff is extremely talented. A special high-five to Lynn Koolish, my developmental editor, whose laughter and gentle prodding kept the assembly line rolling. Thank you so much, Lynn—you are an ace.

… to Steve and Lisa Ferguson, owners of Steve's Sewing Machine Repair in our town, for their incredible response time, on several occasions, when I ran my wonderful sewing machines to exhaustion.

Introduction

In this book are more than 80 quilting patterns, designed in continuous lines. Most of the designs can be stitched in only one line, and each design is accompanied by a directional stitching diagram. All have been designed with the idea of creating the smoothest path possible for quilting. This means eliminating, as much as possible, stopping, securing stitches, and restarting, whether you quilt by hand or machine. *See copyright page permission statement (page 2) for allowable use of these patterns.*

When I use the term machine, I am including domestic sewing machines, mid-arm, longarm, and all varieties in between. All are wonderful pieces of equipment.

In addition to the pages of quilting patterns, there are short sections on machine-quilting techniques, quilt design, and background stitches.

Most of the patterns in this book were printed as large as space and page design allowed. This is because when enlarging or reducing patterns on a copier, enlarging is more likely to cause a slight distortion. See Enlarging and Reducing Patterns (page 107).

Photos of quilted examples of the quilting patterns can be found throughout the book. All of the patterns have at least one stitched example. Use the Easy-Find Design Index (pages 108–110) to find and keep track of your favorite patterns.

Enjoy,

Hari Walner

Free-Motion Quilting Tips

The patterns in this book are intended for use with free-motion quilting techniques, unless you are quilting by hand. These tips are basic. They are, for the most part, of concern to the quilters using a domestic machine. Some tips might be helpful to quilters using longarm machines.

1. Provide a surface at your sewing machine that easily supports your project. You cannot keep control of moving a quilt that insists on falling off the table any-more than you can control when the sun comes up.

2. Use adequate lighting in front of and in back of the needle. Free-motion techniques require you to guide your quilt from front to back, back to front, and side to side while the needle is in motion. Good lighting is a must.

3. Find a free-motion foot for your machine that allows good visibility all around your needle. You often need to see behind your needle while you are stitching.

4. Mark your design clearly. It is imperative when machine quilting to be able to see where you want to stitch (see marking tips, page 106).

5. When you have extra quilt bulk in your machine because of a large project, try to fold the quilt in deep pinch pleats rather than rolling it. A rolled quilt can be cumbersome and tiresome to handle. Office binder clips are great for holding the pleats together.

6. Gather enough of the quilt around the needle so that you only have to move the area of the quilt that you are stitching on. The quilt should be flexible enough so the weight of your hands resting on the quilt will easily guide it under the needle. If you spread the quilt out flat on your sewing table, you will have to move the whole quilt every time you take a stitch.

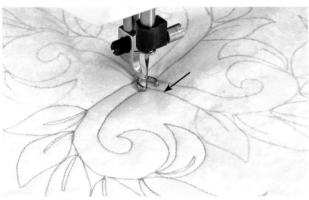

8. Relax and remember to breathe while you are stitching. Holding your breath from anxiety will not help your quilting—your brain and your muscles need the oxygen.

7. Never watch your needle while you are stitching. Instead, watch the line of the design that you are feeding into your needle. Looking 1/8″–1/4″ down the road will help you stay in control.

Warm up. Take a clue from Major League Baseball players. These million-dollar athletes are the best of the best in their field, and yet, before a game they stretch, they throw, they take batting practice. Before you start quilting on a project, loosen up for a few minutes. Make a practice sandwich so you can test the machine and bobbin tension, and find your quilting rhythm. Only then can you do your best work. And don't be too hard on yourself—even these baseball players sometimes strike out. Practice may not ever make us perfect, but it makes us the best we can be.

Design Your Quilt for Quilting

Once you finish a quilt top, it is often difficult to find the right quilting pattern, you set the quilt top aside, and it remains a quilt top. It doesn't reach quilt status.

You can eliminate this roadblock if you make the major decisions—quilting designs, fabric, and technique—before you start to make your quilt.

I design most of my quilts around a quilting pattern, but your inspiration might come from a piecing pattern, a favorite block, a special fabric, or a technique. When you know what look you want for your quilt, you might also consider quilting thread and batting early on in the design process.

Because the quilting comes near the end of the quiltmaking process, it is easy to always put off decisions about how to quilt the top. But if you make these decisions in the beginning, you can proceed with confidence. No longer will you hear that little nagging voice whisper, "How are you going to quilt this, my dear?"

This chapter (pages 8–15) describes the major aspects I consider when beginning to make a new quilt.

Selecting a Quilting Pattern

Many quilting designs are not as difficult to stitch as they look. Before rejecting a design because it looks difficult, please consider the following:

All quilting stitches have one thing in common: This stitch is either there, or it is *not* there. All quilting designs, no matter how simple or complicated they appear, are made up of the same basic idea, individual stitches, one following another—and no individual stitch is more difficult to execute than another stitch. How you put each stitch in line with other stitches determines what your quilting design looks like.

The following is an example of how the concept of individual stitches can be used to understand the simplicity or complexity of quilting designs.

I have always thought that the most difficult motif to free-motion flawlessly is a *perfect* circle. It looks so simple, but it is one long, smooth line whose beginning and ending stitches must match up. When stitching a circle, any stitch that is slightly out of line will show instantly and, because a circle is such a common visual, slight drifting off the line is obvious.

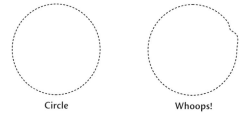

Circle   Whoops!

Depending on the size of your circle (the larger, the more challenging), you may have to pause your stitching several times to reposition your hands to help guide your quilt, and each time you must pause in the middle of an arc because there is no rest stop. Then you need to restart stitching again while trying to keep the arc smooth. With practice, of course, you will master this, but it does take practice.

Now, twist that circle into a figure 8. This is a bit more complicated looking, but now there is a logical place to pause (where the lines cross) and reposition your hands.

Twist into a figure 8.

Duplicate the figure 8 and turn it 90°. The design becomes more interesting, and it is easier to stitch than the circle because you have a *rest stop.*

Add another figure 8.   When you add more lines, you add more rest stops.

Because there may be more stitches in a fancier design, it will probably take a little *longer* to mark and to stitch, but it does not make it *harder* to stitch. Designs that offer places to stop so you can move your hand position(s), and allow you to give a thought about how to proceed next, can be just as easy, or easier, to stitch as simple-looking designs.

Although there are exceptions (designs that require a great deal of backtracking over previous stitches, such as traditional feather-type designs, require more experience and control), the difference between a more complicated design and a simple design is usually just the length of the line.

Eliminate Seams When Possible

You can often redraft blocks to eliminate seamlines so they don't interfere with your quilting design. Here are two examples.

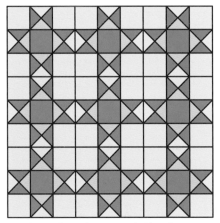

1a. This traditional Nine-Patch Ohio Star is assembled into a quilt top *block by block.* You can see that the largest squares and the smallest squares have seams that could detract from your quilting.

1b. By redrafting the block and assembling the quilt top *row by row,* you eliminate the seams that might detract from your quilting.

1c. You now have more freedom in selecting quilting designs because the seamline ceases to be a concern.

2a. Many blocks are constructed in this 8-pointed star configuration, but they are assembled *block by block.* Again the seams detract from your quilting designs.

2b. If you redraft these star patterns, you can eliminate many seams, although the quilt top takes a bit longer to assemble because of the extra set-in patches.

2c. Set-in seams can be a challenge, since you invest a good deal of time when constructing blocks like this, but they are worth doing because of how much prettier your quilting looks. There are many excellent teachers and good books that can help you if you have problems with set-in seams.

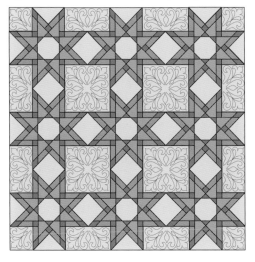

PRESS SEAMS OPEN

When you cannot eliminate a seam in an area to be quilted, press your seam allowances open instead of to one side. This will create a smoother surface for free-motion quilting.

Selecting Fabric

When you decide to stitch pretty quilting designs in your quilt, you want them to be visible. In the beginning, when planning your piecing, take into consideration the exact fabric that you will use in the patches where these quilting designs will be.

Consider also the kind of wear and upkeep (cleaning?) your quilt will need, and select a fabric that is suitable. An endless variety is available.

The simple examples below use the same quilting design, stitched on different types of fabric. More examples can be seen throughout this book.

Light and medium solid fabrics show your quilting very well. The lighter fabrics make it easy to mark a design, and you can see the marked designs easily while quilting.

Tone-on-tone fabrics can add a great deal of interest to your quilt while still allowing your quilting to show. Many batik-type fabrics show quilting nicely.

Dark solid fabrics often look beautiful and dramatic when quilted with lighter threads. It can sometimes take a little more time marking a dark fabric, but it is worth the extra effort.

Unless you are using a rope for thread, don't worry about stitching fancy quilting designs on a busy print. Your quilting won't be seen—and it is very difficult to find needles large enough for a rope.

Think About Threads

Left to right:
Top row: 100-wt. silk, 50-wt. cotton, 40-wt. polyester

Middle row: 40-wt. rayon, 30-wt. cotton, 12-wt. cotton

Bottom row: 30-wt. variegated polyester, 40-wt. variegated cotton, nylon invisible

A great selection of threads is available to us: exquisite silk and cotton; beautiful polyester and rayon; heavy cottons that give a rich, embroidered look; versatile invisible nylon; and a huge selection of specialty threads.

Small stitches and delicate designs call for thinner threads. Quilts that will withstand heavy use need sturdy threads. Many threads can satisfy both the aesthetic and the utilitarian needs of our projects.

Make a stitched sample with your thread to see if it serves your purpose. The following examples show how different a design can look depending on the thread used. This moon design was stitched with nine different threads.

Batting

Whether you want natural or synthetic materials, are concerned about allergies, like a low loft or a puffy look, are a hand quilter or a machine quilter, there is a batt for your every purpose and desired result.

Read what the manufacturers say on their packaging. There is a great deal of useful information on the package as to what the batt is made of, washability, shrinkage, warmth, and how dense quilting should be for stability. The maker of the batt wants to give you useful information so your project will be successful.

Preshrinking is not necessary with most batts, and some manufacturers recommend against it for certain batts. If you like slight shrinkage for an antique look, you probably will not want to preshrink your batts, because they will shrink when the quilt is first wet and dried.

I preshrink almost all of the batts I use. Except for the two synthetic batts, the batts below were preshrunk before they were quilted for the examples. If you want to preshrink your batt, follow the manufacturer's instructions.

The photos below show six different batts that have been stitched using the same fabric, thread, and quilting design. It is difficult to discern the subtle differences in photos, but there is often a great deal of difference as to how the quilt feels with different methods of quilting.

Experiment with several batts in small projects to find out what will fill your needs and give you the most pleasure.

Wool—100% wool

Cotton—100% cotton

Bamboo—50% bamboo, 50% cotton

Silk—90% silk, 10% cotton

Green—100% recycled plastic bottles

High loft polyester—100% polyester

Borders

If you want to quilt a design in your border, let your choice of border quilting designs determine the style of border piecing. Here are three commonly pieced border styles that I have found very useful.

Overlapping Edges

This is the simplest border to attach to your quilt. Use this border when your border quilting design is stronger in one direction (horizontal or vertical) than in the other, or when you want individual quilting motifs to face the same direction.

Because of this border's simplicity, it is often used on utilitarian quilts.

Mitered Corners

If your border quilt design finishes on a diagonal up toward the corner, you can use mitered corners because the seamline will not interfere with the quilt design.

Squared Corners

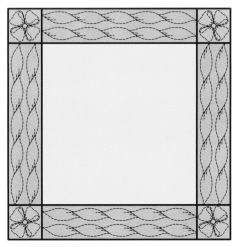

If the border corner quilting element is a long motif, it may be better off isolated in a setting square. This piecing is handy if the seams do not compete with either the corner or the side border quilting motifs. If the square is made from a different fabric, it adds another graphic element to the quilt.

Diagonal Corners

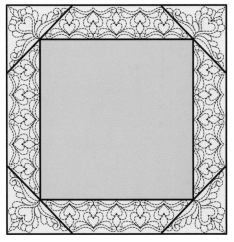

This is a terrific border corner if you have a graceful corner motif that begs not to have to fight a seamline in the corner. Because the corner patch doesn't have a seam going to the corner, or a horizontal or vertical seam that can cut through a design, the quilting motif is not interrupted. Simple assembly directions are on the next page.

Triangle Border Corners

This is a simple border to create, and it avoids seamlines that might detract from your quilting. You don't have to worry about mitering the corner, and the edge is always on the straight of grain.

Add the Border Edges

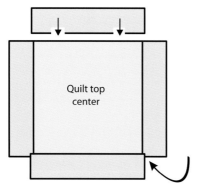

After the borders are sewn on, there will be a ¼˝ overlap in the corners because of the seam allowance.

Measure the edges of your quilt top, and cut the border to that exact length. Sew each of the four borders to the edge of the quilt as shown. This will leave the corners open.

Make the Corners

To determine the size of the triangle corners:

1. Double the width of your border (finished), and add 1⅛˝.

   Example: If the finished width of the border is 4˝:
   $$4˝ \times 2 = 8˝ \quad 8˝ + 1⅛˝ = 9⅛˝$$

Cut squares border width × 2 + 1⅛˝.

2. Cut 2 squares the size you determined above.

Squares cut on diagonal to make 4 triangles

3. Cut these 2 squares on the diagonal. You now have 4 triangles.

Mark the Corners

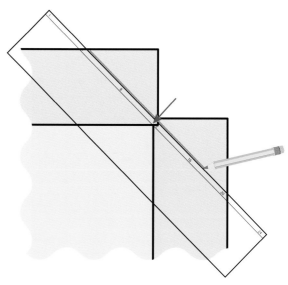

1. Place a ruler at a 45° angle from the border seams. Let the ¼˝ line on your ruler sit directly on the stitched corner that the 2 side borders have made.

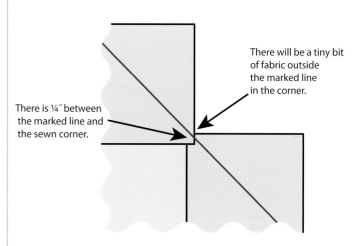

There is ¼˝ between the marked line and the sewn corner.

There will be a tiny bit of fabric outside the marked line in the corner.

Marked corner

2. Draw a line all the way across the 2 borders. The line will go through the tiny overlap that was created when you first attached the borders.

Attach the Corners

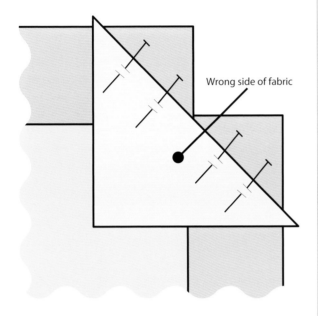

Wrong side of fabric

1. With the right sides of the fabric together, place a triangle in a corner. Center the edge of the long side of the triangle on the marked line. The corners of the triangle will extend beyond the side borders. Pin a triangle to all 4 corners.

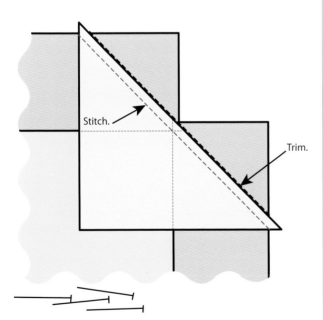

Stitch.

Trim.

2. Stitch the corner to the quilt top. Use a ¼″ seam allowance. Trim away background after stitching.

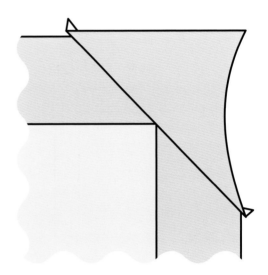

3. Fold the triangle to the corner. It will be a bit larger than the rest of the border.

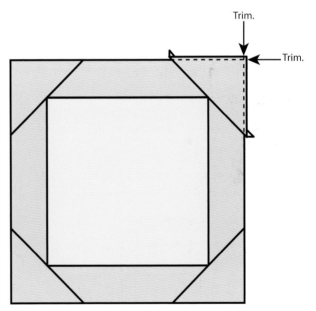

Trim.

Trim.

4. Press and trim the edges of the corner even with the rest of the border.

Continuous-Line Patterns

CAMELOT

Pattern: page 17
Fabric: Cotton
Thread: Cotton 50-weight

Camelot Stitching Diagram

Follow the arrows in the diagram with your finger before you stitch this design. Once you see how easily it is done, you will be able to stitch with confidence.

The center line is stitched separately. The corners of the center line should be stitched up to, but not over, the line that is the main motif.

For the main design, begin and finish stitching at the •, taking care to follow the arrows that lead to the motifs in the corners.

Center line should stop here in each corner.

Pattern: *7˝ × 7˝* • **Stitched example:** page 99

Madrigal Stitching Diagrams

Begin stitching at the •, and follow the arrows. When you get to a flower, be sure to follow the arrows and stitch the center of the flower first. This will help avoid puckering in the center of the flower.

Madrigal will lend a graceful rhythm to your quilting projects.

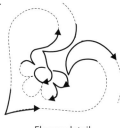

Flower detail

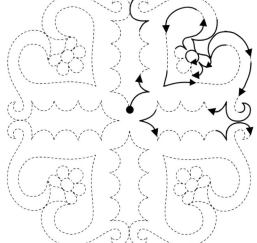

Block: 5½″ × 5½″ • Border: 3″ • Repeat: 2½″
Stitched examples: page 100

Repeat

Border

Note: The corner tulip leaves and connectors are slightly different from the other motifs.

Dutch Romance Stitching Diagrams

For both block and border you may begin stitching anywhere. Just follow the arrows, and you will finish back where you started.

Block

Continuous-Line Patterns

19

Sunny Flowers Stitching Diagrams

Block

Begin at the •, and follow the arrows. Stitch the center of each flower before stitching that flower's petals. The arrows lead you to the next flower.

Extension used at corners

Repeat

Border

Follow the arrows, and stitch the center of each flower before you stitch its petals. You only need to travel around the border once with this design.

Floral Galaxy Stitching Diagrams

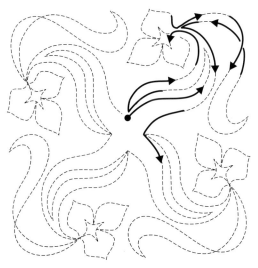

Begin stitching at the •, near the center of the design. Stitch the small inner curves first, and then stitch the line that leads to the flower.

The flower detail drawing shows how to stitch the flower and get back to the flowing lines of the galaxy. The design is continuous, so you will finish where you started.

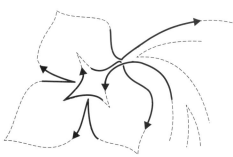

Flower detail

Lavender Blues *Border*

Border: 3″ · **Repeat:** 2½″ · **Stitched example:** page 66

See the matching block on page 23.

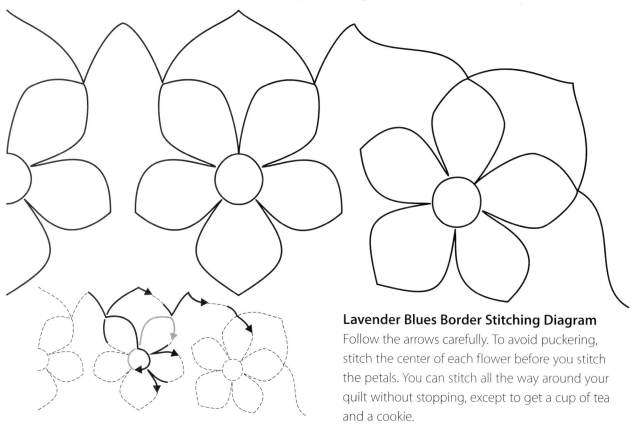

Lavender Blues Border Stitching Diagram

Follow the arrows carefully. To avoid puckering, stitch the center of each flower before you stitch the petals. You can stitch all the way around your quilt without stopping, except to get a cup of tea and a cookie.

Floral Galaxy *Border*

Border: 2½″ · **Repeat** 2½″ · **Stitched example:** page 66

See the matching block on page 21.

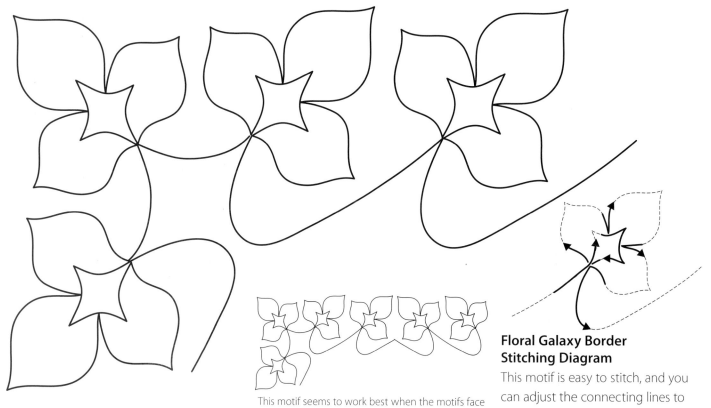

This motif seems to work best when the motifs face each other in the center of the border.

Floral Galaxy Border Stitching Diagram

This motif is easy to stitch, and you can adjust the connecting lines to fit your border. Follow the arrows.

Lavender Blues Stitching Diagram

Begin stitching at the • and stitch toward the 1, to the center of the first flower. Complete the center circle, and follow the arrows to stitch each petal. After stitching each flower, follow the arrows, and use the inner line to get to the next flower.

After you have stitched all the flowers and the inner line, follow the arrows, and complete the outer line.

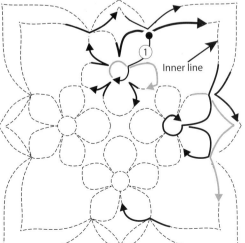

April Delight
Stitching Diagrams

Block

This graceful little block is easy to stitch and is very useful.

Border

Follow the arrows. The lines that connect the motifs at the corners are slightly different from the other connecting lines. Begin anywhere.

Repeat

Optional: **Heart in the Corner**

If you would like to fill the corners of a square patch, add this heart to each corner, and follow the stitching diagram for the corner heart.

Optional corner heart stitching

Nosegay Stitching Diagram

This design fills a circular or a square area. Begin stitching at •, and follow the arrows.

TIP

When faced with long, gentle curves, such as those in Daisy Ballet, don't be intimidated. Consider these ideas:

- Pause your stitching at the beginning of the long curve. Use the needle-down feature if you have it.
- Position your hands so you won't have to reposition them while stitching the curve, and try to stitch the entire curve without stopping. If you do stop, do not let the fabric move. Needle down might help.
- Take an extra breath. Don't forget to breathe while stitching.
- Don't look at your needle while stitching. Look at the design line that you are feeding into the needle.

Daisy Ballet Stitching Diagram
Begin stitching at the •, and follow the arrows.

See the matching block on page 26.

Border Motif
The repeat is between each •.

This is where the
motifs meet at
the corners.

For convenience, this is
the assembled corner.

Border diagram with
repeated motifs

Daisy Ballet Border Stitching Diagram
You can begin stitching anywhere on this
border, but I like to start at the dots. Follow
the arrows, and you only have to go around
your quilt once.

Colorado Springtime Stitching Diagram

Begin stitching at the •, and stitch toward the center of the block. Follow the arrows around the center motif as shown, and then let the thick gray arrow lead you to a corner motif. Follow these arrows to stitch the four corner motifs until you arrive back at the •. Continue to follow the arrows, and stitch the remaining line that takes you to the points on the outside center of the block.

Starshine Stitching Diagram

Begin at the •, and stitch the circle first. Follow the arrows, and finish stitching at the •.

Border: 4″ • **Repeat:** 4″ • **Stitched example:** page 72

See the matching block on page 31.

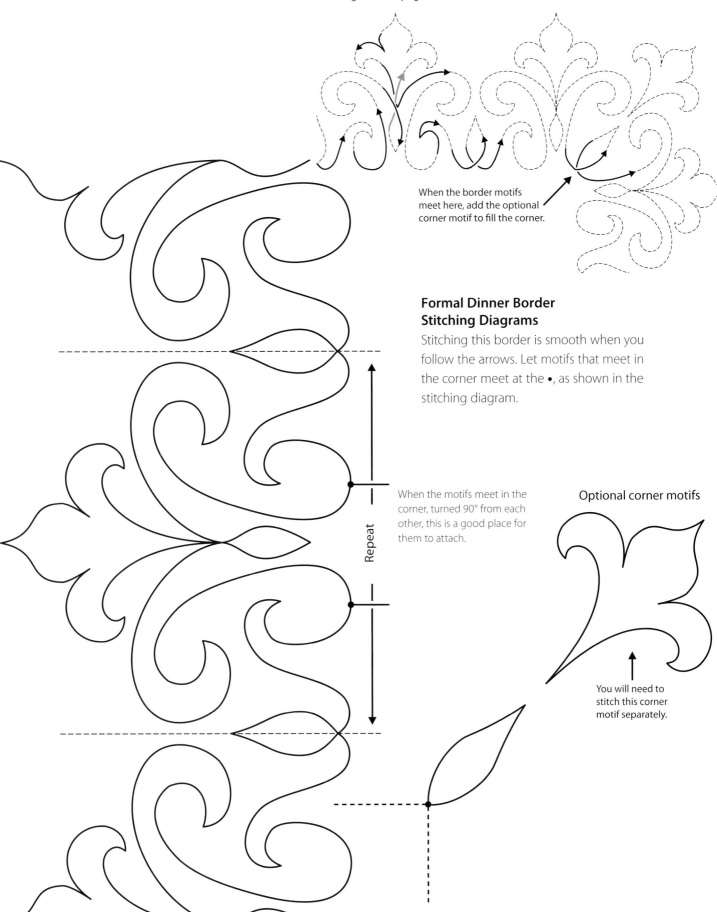

When the border motifs meet here, add the optional corner motif to fill the corner.

Formal Dinner Border Stitching Diagrams

Stitching this border is smooth when you follow the arrows. Let motifs that meet in the corner meet at the •, as shown in the stitching diagram.

When the motifs meet in the corner, turned 90° from each other, this is a good place for them to attach.

Repeat

Optional corner motifs

You will need to stitch this corner motif separately.

See the matching border on page 30.

Formal Dinner Stitching Diagram

Follow these arrows carefully. Begin stitching at •, and stitch toward the corner motif. After you have stitched the small pointed loop, be sure to follow the arrow that takes you up into the fleur-de-lis motif.

If you would like this pattern for a large block, use 4 Molly's Tulips, as shown. Stitch 1 motif at a time.

Molly's Tulips Stitching Diagram

Begin stitching at •, and follow the arrows carefully. There are 2 places where you will need to stitch back over a few stitches: One is at the throat of the heart, and one is at the base of the flower. You will finish stitching at the •.

Begin stitching here.

Simple Melody Stitching Diagram

Begin stitching at the •, and follow the arrows. Finish where the diagram indicates. I embroider the eye rather than make it a quilting stitch. This warbler is a pretty motif for many projects.

Sleepy Time Stitching Diagram

Begin stitching Sleepy Time at the •, and follow the arrows. Stitch the star first, and then the moon. You will finish stitching where you started.

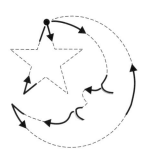

Catnap Stitching Diagrams

Catnap, unlike her friend Foxy Feline, needs 2 lines to complete the design. Stitch the face first, beginning at the •, and ending at the ■.

Next, begin stitching the body at the • in the whole body diagram. For the double lines that define the feet, stitch closely parallel to each other or back-stitch on top of previous stitches.

End face here.

Begin face here.

Face detail

End body here.

Begin body here.

Foxy Feline Stitching Diagrams

Stitch Foxy Feline's face first, beginning at the •. When you get back to the •, follow the arrows down into her body. You will finish stitching where indicated.

Begin here.

Face detail

End here.

Merry Mouse Stitching Diagram

You may want to embroider the eye before quilting Merry Mouse. Begin stitching at the •, and follow the arrows. The dashed line next to a line means that you will stitch right next to, or over, those stitches. You will finish where you started.

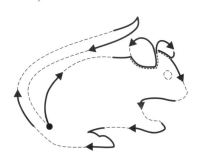

Extend line here
to add length
to border.

Butterfly Beauties Border Stitching Diagram

If your border goes all the way around your project, begin stitching anywhere, and follow the arrows. You will finish where you began.

If your border is in shorter segments, begin stitching at an end motif, and follow the arrows.

This border turns the corner easily.

Repeat

See the matching border on page 36.

Butterfly Beauties Stitching Diagrams

With this block design, begin stitching anywhere, and follow the arrows. You will finish where you began.

With the center flower motif, begin at the • , and stitch the center of the flower first; then stitch the petals.

Summer Leaves Border Stitching Diagrams

Begin stitching at a •, and follow the arrows. Stitch the vein of the leaf before stitching the outline of the leaf.

If the design goes continuously around your project, you will finish stitching where you started.

Leaf Stitching Options

Option 1: When stitching the vein, stitch back directly on top of your previous stitches for the appearance of one line.

Option 2: Stitch right next to the drawn line going into the leaf, and next to the other side of the line going back.

Option 1   Or   Option 2

Corner   Middle

Basic motif

Note that the lines that connect the leaves in the middle of a border and the ones that connect the leaves in the corners are slightly different from the basic motif.

Pattern: *7˝ × 7˝* • **Stitched example:** page 101

See a compatible border (Summer Leaves) on page 38.

End.

Begin.

Close Harmony Stitching Diagram

Begin at the •, and finish where indicated. The arrows show how to stitch in a continuous line.

Note: Where there is a thin, gray dotted line, you will be stitching back over some of your previous stitches. This is easier to do if you remember not to look at your needle. Instead, look at the stitches you want to stitch on top of.

Before you stitch the leaves, check out the Leaf Stitching Options on the facing page.

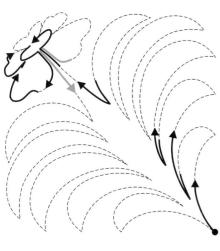

Ground Cover Stitching Diagram

Begin stitching at the •, and follow the arrows. When you arrive at the flower, stitch the entire center before stitching the petals—this helps avoid puckering. Follow the arrows to stitch the other side of the design.

This design can also be used for much larger blocks. Because of the way the pattern meets in the centers, the design with the flowers in the center is slightly larger than the one with the flowers in the corner. Stitch one motif at a time.

Venetian Waves Stitching Diagram

This graceful design is very useful when you want to add movement to the lines in your quilt.

Begin stitching at the •, and follow the arrows.

This corner flower is slightly smaller than the other 7-petaled flowers.

Bonny Blooms Border Stitching Diagram

On some designs, like this one, you can begin stitching anywhere. When that is the case, I like to begin at an inconspicuous place so tiny securing stitches are less likely to show.

Follow the arrows in the diagram, and when you come to the 7-petaled flower, stitch the entire center before stitching the petals.

Bonny Blooms Stitching Diagrams

Oh yes, you can! Begin at the •, and first stitch the 2 center lines (1 and 2) as shown in the detail. Then cross over, and sew up into the side floral segment. Follow line 3 to a corner flower. Line 3 will take you from flower to flower. You will finish stitching where you began.

Corner flower detail

#1
#2
#3

Do-Si-Do Stitching Diagram

This design gives the illusion of movement in the center, and it is easy to follow the arrows. You may begin stitching anywhere, but I like to begin stitching at the • because it is easier to hide beginning and ending securing stitches.

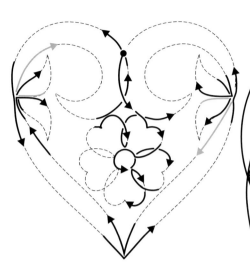

Candy Box Stitching Diagram

Begin stitching at the •, and follow the arrows down to the flower. The arrows will lead you to stitch the center of the flower first and then the petals. Follow the arrows around the inside line of the heart to the leaves. When you arrive back at the •, follow the arrows to stitch the outside line of the heart.

This block is 4 of the Candy Box heart motifs pointing toward the center.

When using this motif as the center of the large block made with 4 motifs, check to make sure the larger loops are oriented correctly.

Optional center motif

This block is 4 of the Candy Box heart motifs and the optional center motif. The motifs as shown would make a 10″ block if you let the heart motifs touch where indicated.

Motifs touch here.

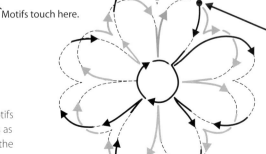

Optional: Center Motif Stitching Diagram

Begin at the •, and follow the arrows toward the center. Stitch the circle first and then the larger outer loops. When you get back to the •, follow the gray arrows to stitch the smaller inner loops. You will finish at the •.

Pattern: 4½″ × 4½″ • **Stitched example:** page 80

Dahlia Dandy Stitching Diagram

Begin stitching at the •, and stitch the circle first. Continue to follow the arrows to stitch the petals. You will finish stitching at the •.

Lovely Lily

Pattern: 4½″ × 4½″ • **Stitched example:** page 80

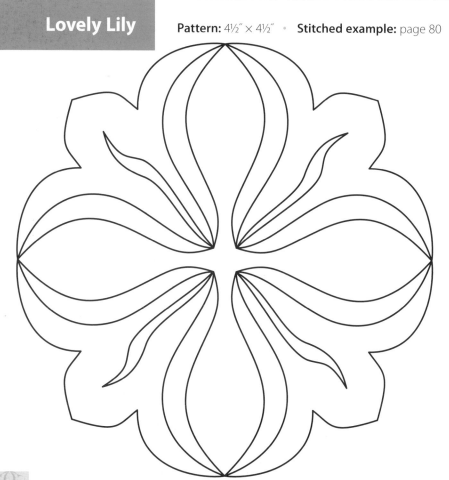

Lovely Lily Stitching Diagram

Begin stitching at the •. Stitch toward the center of the design, and follow the arrows to stitch each flower and stamen. You will finish stitching where you began.

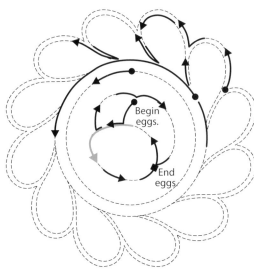

Little Feathered Nest Stitching Diagram

It takes 4 lines to stitch this design, but 2 of them are optional. When stitching the eggs, you will need to backtrack over a few previous stitches.

The larger circle and the line of feathers are stitched in 1 line. The optional inner circle and the outer accent line surrounding the feathers are separate lines.

Stitch the egg line first, then the smaller inner circle, the circle with the feathers and, if you like, the outer line. Follow the arrows.

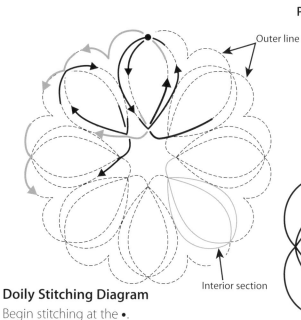

Doily Stitching Diagram

Begin stitching at the •.

Except for the first ⅛ Doily section, stitch each complete interior section before moving on to the next. Follow the arrows, and you will see that you use the center curved line to move from section to section. Complete the first section after the others are stitched.

When the interior sections are complete, you'll be back at the •. Then stitch the outer surrounding line.

One-Line Samba Stitching Diagrams

Add rhythm to that quilt for your favorite music lover. Begin anywhere, and follow the arrows.

Sweet Adeline Stitching Diagram

Follow these arrows carefully, especially when you reach the corner heart. Begin and finish stitching at the •.

Friendship Stitching Diagram

The Friendship design is one continuous line that is stitched one-eighth of the design at a time. Each segment consists of an inner heart, the pair of leaves, an outer heart, and the flower. Each section flows easily into the next section.

Begin and finish stitching at the •.

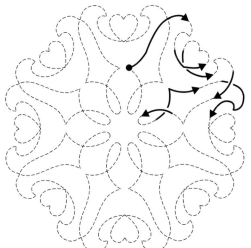

Aphrodite Stitching Diagram

Follow the arrows to stitch Aphrodite in one continuous line. Begin and finish stitching at the •.

Aphrodite was the Greek goddess of love.

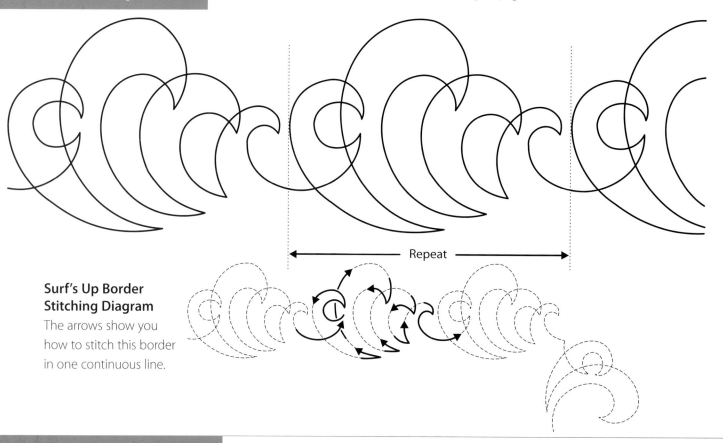

Repeat

Surf's Up Border Stitching Diagram

The arrows show you how to stitch this border in one continuous line.

Night Light *Border*   **Border:** 3″ · **Stitched example:** page 76

Night Light Border Stitching Diagram

It is easier to stitch straight lines when free-motion quilting if you remember to look at the line you are feeding into the needle and not at your needle. Don't hesitate at the points. Follow the arrows around your quilt. A star fills the corner nicely.

Night-lights can be so comforting.

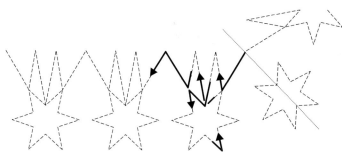

Simply Swirls Stitching Diagram

Begin stitching at the •, and follow the arrows. You will finish stitching at the •.

Placement

When marking this design in a square, align the design vertically and horizontally along the axes as shown.

Pattern: 6½˝ × 6½˝ • **Stitched example:** page 75

See a compatible border (Dutch Romance) on page 19.

Note: Each heart and stem section is stitched the same way.

Spring Basket Stitching Diagram

Stitch the heart on the basket first (Line 1).

Begin Line 2 at the • where indicated, and follow the arrows to complete the basket, bouquet, and basket handle.

Line 3 is a simple line to complete the basket base.

Begin Line 2.

End Line 2.

Line 1

Line 3

Elegance Stitching Diagrams

Block

Begin stitching at the •, and follow the arrows. Simply elegant!

Border

Start at the beginning of your border. If the border goes all the way around your project, you may start anywhere. Follow the arrows.

Stitch each corner heart with one line.

Pattern: 6½˝ × 6½˝ • **Stitched example:** page 71

Deco Delight Stitching Diagrams

This design and the design on the facing page require confidence and concentration. There are several times when it will help to slow down. The Deco Delight block is stitched one half at a time, divided on the diagonal.

Begin at the •, the base of the smallest oval, and stitch that oval. Slow down when you approach where the ovals meet. When you finish that smallest oval, stop, and take 1 tiny stitch the width of your thread straight down toward the base of the next biggest oval. Stitch close lines right next to each other, not on top of each other. (Look at the enlarged detail.)

When all 5 ovals are completed, take a tiny stitch again, and follow the arrows to stitch the line of one side of the outer swirls. Begin stitching the swirls on the other side where shown on the diagram.

Crescent Charm Stitching Diagram

Begin stitching at the •. Follow the arrow up toward the crescent and back down toward the first inner arc on the left. Leave enough room at the base of each arc for the other lines that will follow. Stitch these lines right next to, but not on top of, the adjacent line. After you stitch the two arcs on the left, follow the arrow and travel ¼ of the circle to the next group of arcs. Stitch the outer arc on the right first, then the inner arc on the right, and follow the arrows to the crescent. Then stitch the left side. Stitch slowly where you need to. *Remember:* This is machine quilting, not machine racing.

If you follow the arrows in this manner, you will finish stitching the design where you began.

TIP

Because of the places where 6 lines of stitching are right n xt to each other, it helps to make a little practice sample with the thread you intend to use. Stitch six 1″ lines directly next to each other but not touching. You will find that you need to allow more space for thick threads and less for thin threads.

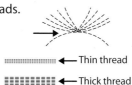

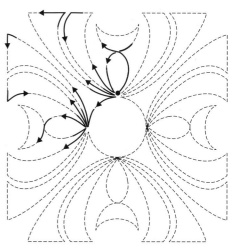

Border 1: 2″ • **Border 2:** 1⅝″ • **Stitched examples:** page 71

See the matching block on page 59.

Border 1

Aztec Border 1 Stitching Diagram

Begin stitching at one end of a motif, and stitch the line with the sun (half circle) first. Go back to the beginning on the middle line. Then stitch the top line, and go on to the next motif. Continue around your border.

Second time around

Aztec Border 2 Stitching Diagram

Because the Aztec 2 border design eliminates one line of pointed rays, the easiest way to stitch this border is to stitch one line at a time all the way around your project, and stitch the second line a second time around. The inner border lines do not touch at the corners.

Border 2

See the matching borders on page 58.

Aztec Stitching Diagrams

Aztec is fun to stitch. There are 2 continuous lines in this block, each with a half circle. Begin at the innermost •, and stitch the inner line with the points first. When you get back to the •, stitch the line with the inner half circle.

Begin at the outer • for the second line. You can stitch the outer line the same way as the inner line (by going around the block 3 times),

or you can stitch each side separately and still keep it a continuous line, like Border 1 on the facing page.

Both lines begin and finish at the •. See outer line detail.

Outer line detail (for stitching one side motif at a time)

Rodeo Stitching Diagram

Begin stitching at the •, and follow the black arrows. Stitch the entire center line first, and then stitch the inner loops.

To avoid confusion, after you have finished the inner loops, follow the gray arrows to stitch the larger loop line.

The outer line is stitched separately. If you prefer a simpler design, you can eliminate this outer line.

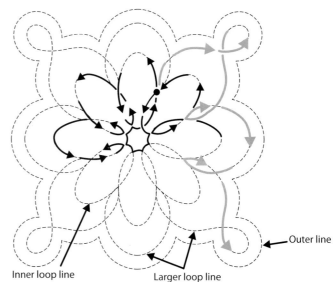

Inner loop line

Larger loop line

Outer line

Old Oak Stitching Diagrams

You can begin stitching anywhere, but I have marked a • for a starting point. Follow the arrows.

Backtrack a few stitches in details where the roots meet the trunk (see root detail).

The veins in the leaves can also be backtracked, or you can stitch right next to the vein line going in and stitch next to the other side of the line going out.

Knot detail

Leaf detail

Root detail

Border: *2″* • **Stitched examples:** page 73

See the matching block on page 63.

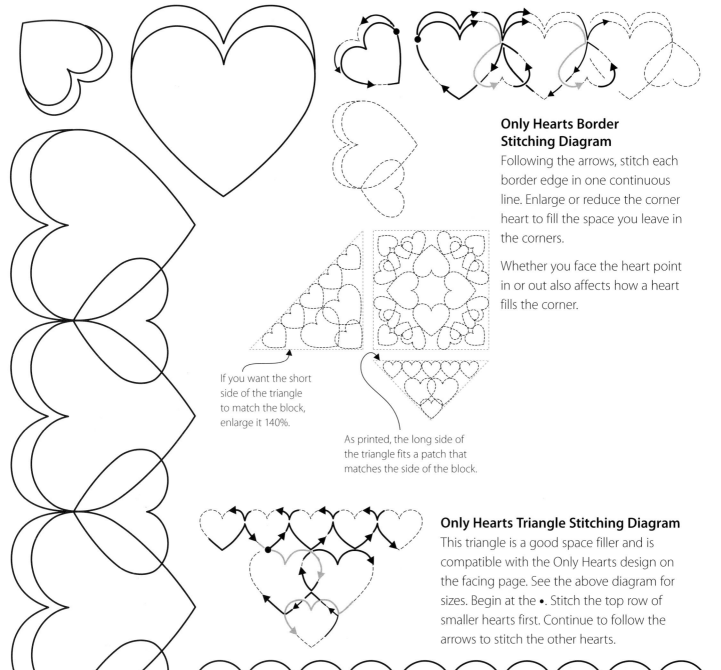

Only Hearts Border Stitching Diagram

Following the arrows, stitch each border edge in one continuous line. Enlarge or reduce the corner heart to fill the space you leave in the corners.

Whether you face the heart point in or out also affects how a heart fills the corner.

If you want the short side of the triangle to match the block, enlarge it 140%.

As printed, the long side of the triangle fits a patch that matches the side of the block.

Only Hearts Triangle Stitching Diagram

This triangle is a good space filler and is compatible with the Only Hearts design on the facing page. See the above diagram for sizes. Begin at the •. Stitch the top row of smaller hearts first. Continue to follow the arrows to stitch the other hearts.

See the matching border and triangle on page 62.

See the matching border and triangle on page 62.

TIP

There are several times in this pattern where arrows get to an undefined point (areas marked with a tiny dashed line). It helps to mark these areas on your project so you don't accidentally go too far the first time you get to one of these areas. When you first come to this kind of inter-section, turn back as shown. Then, when you come back to that area, slow down and stitch right up to, but not over, the point that was already stitched. Turn and continue to follow the arrows.

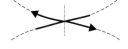

Only Hearts Stitching Diagram

Follow the arrows carefully to stitch this design in one line. After stitching the inner line as shown, you will stitch a corner group of hearts. Then you will travel a line of a large heart to get to the next corner group of hearts.

Eye detail

Splendid Swan Stitching Diagrams

Splendid Swan is designed to be used on point (a square turned 45°), but it can be used in many ways.

Begin stitching anywhere on the design. There are 2 crossovers in the tail feathers, and the eye is detailed for clarity.

SPLENDID SWAN

Fabric: Cotton **Thread:** Rayon (design),
Cotton/polyester blend (background)
Batt: Wool **Pattern:** page 64

SURF'S UP
Pattern: page 52

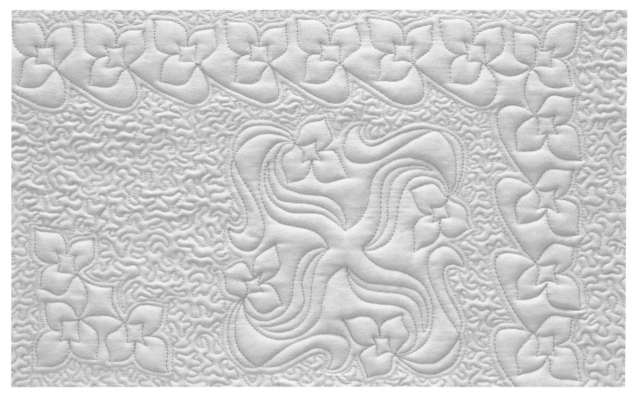

FLORAL GALAXY

Fabric: Cotton sateen   **Batt:** Wool   **Thread:** Cotton (design), Silk (background)

Patterns: page 21 (block), page 22 (border)

LAVENDER BLUES

Fabric: Cotton sateen   **Batt:** Bamboo   **Thread:** Polyester (design), Silk (background)

Patterns: page 22 (border), page 23 (block)

SAY IT WITH FLOWERS
Fabric: Cotton **Batt:** Polyester
Thread: Cotton **Pattern:** page 93

STARSHINE
Fabric: Polyester **Batt:** Polyester
Thread: Rayon (design), Silk (background)
Pattern: page 29

BUTTERFLY BEAUTIES
Fabric: Cotton **Batt:** Polyester
Thread: Polyester (design),
Silk (background)
Patterns: page 36 (border),
page 37 (block)

SPRING BOUQUET

Fabric: 60/40 Cotton/silk blend   **Batt:** Bamboo   **Thread:** Rayon (design), Silk (background)

Patterns: page 82 (block), page 83 (border)

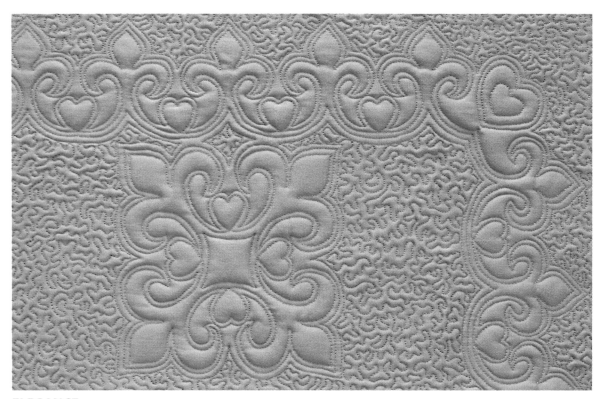

ELEGANCE

Fabric: Cotton sateen   **Batt:** Wool   **Thread:** Rayon (design), Cotton (background)

Pattern: page 55

FEATHERED FRIEND / FRESH FLOWER
Fabric: Polyester/silkie   **Batt:** Wool   **Thread:** Cotton (design), Silk (background)
Patterns: page 95

DOILY
Fabric: 60/40 Cotton/silk blend   **Batt:** Wool
Thread: Polyester (design), Silk (background)
Pattern: page 47

LITTLE FEATHERED NEST
Fabric: Cotton flannel   **Batt:** Wool
Thread: Cotton
Pattern: page 47

MERMAID TRIANGLE
Fabric: Cotton   **Batt:** 80/20 Cotton/polyester
Thread: Rayon (design), Silk (background)
Pattern: page 91

POET TRIANGLE
Fabric: Polyester/silkie   **Batt:** 50/50 Bamboo/sotton
Thread: Rayon (design), Cotton (background)
Pattern: page 91

SUPREME COURTING
Fabric: Silk   **Batt:** Silk   **Thread:** Cotton (design), Silk (background)
Patterns: page 86 (border), page 87 (block)

DECO DELIGHT
Fabric: Cotton (hand-dyed),
Batt: 50/50 Bamboo/cotton
Thread: Cotton (design),
Silk (background)
Pattern: page 56

CRESCENT CHARM
Fabric: Polyester/silkie
Batt: 50/50 Cotton/silk
Thread: Rayon (design),
Silk (background)
Pattern: page 57

AZTEC BORDERS
Pattern: page 58

AZTEC
Fabric: Cotton (hand-dyed)   **Batt:** Silk
Thread: Cotton
Pattern: page 59

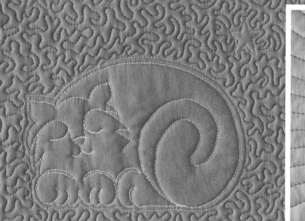

FOXY FELINE
Fabric: Cotton   **Batt:** Silk   **Thread:** Cotton
Pattern: page 35
MERRY MOUSE
Pattern: page 35

SLEEPY TIME
Fabric: Cotton   **Batt:** Recycled plastic bottles
Thread: Cotton (design), Silk (background)
Pattern: page 34

CATNAP
Pattern: page 34

FORMAL DINNER
Fabric: Cotton
Batt: 80/20 Cotton/polyester
Thread: Cotton
Patterns: page 30 (border),
page 31 (block)

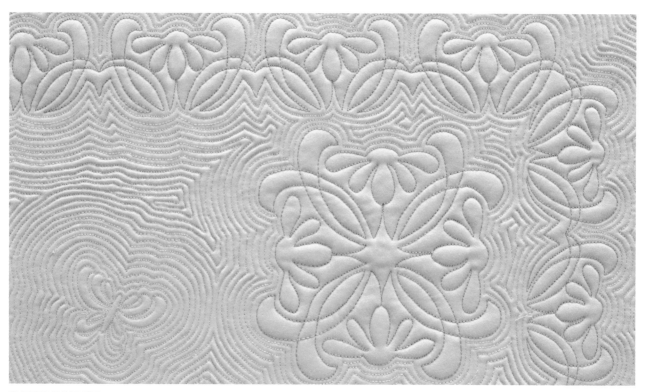

DAISY BALLET
Fabric: Cotton sateen   **Batt:** Wool   **Thread:** Cotton
Patterns: page 26 (block), page 27 (border)

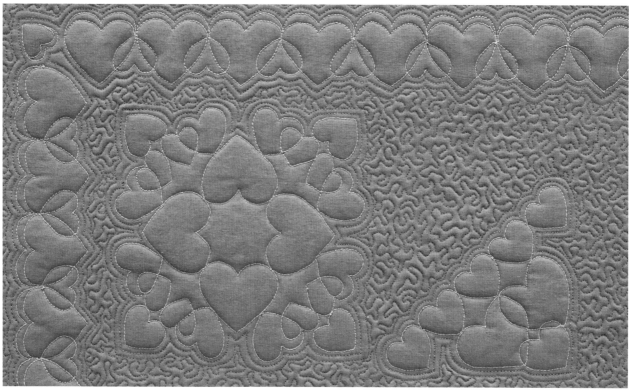

ONLY HEARTS
Fabric: Cotton   **Batt:** Wool   **Thread:** Cotton (design), Silk (background)
Patterns: page 62 (border and triangle), page 63 (block)

FRIENDSHIP
Fabric: Cotton   **Batt:** Silk   **Thread:** Cotton
Pattern: page 50

SONGBIRD TREE
Fabric: Silk   **Batt:** Silk
Thread: Rayon (design), Silk (background)
Pattern: page 85

RIBBON GALAXY
Fabric: Cotton   **Batt:** 80/20 Cotton/polyester
Thread: Polyester (design), variety (background)
Pattern: page 90

DELICIOUS
Fabric: Cotton   **Batt:** Wool
Thread: Rayon (design), Silk (background)
Pattern: page 88

SPRING BASKET
Fabric: Cotton sateen   **Batt:** Wool
Thread: Polyester
Pattern: page 54

APRIL DELIGHT
Fabric: Silk   **Batt:** 50/50 Bamboo/cotton
Thread: Rayon (design), Silk (background)
Pattern: page 24

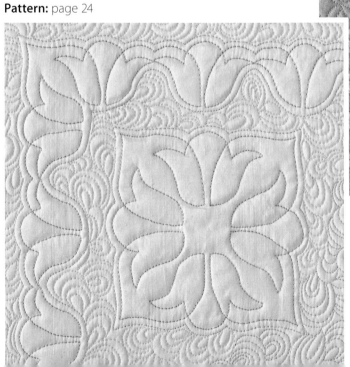

CANDY BOX
Fabric: Cotton   **Batt:** 80/20 Cotton/polyester
Thread: Cotton
Pattern: page 45

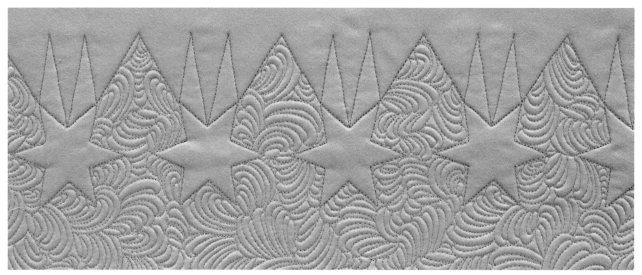

NIGHT LIGHT
Fabric: Cotton sateen   **Batt:** Recycled plastic bottles   **Thread:** Cotton (design), Silk (background)
Pattern: page 52

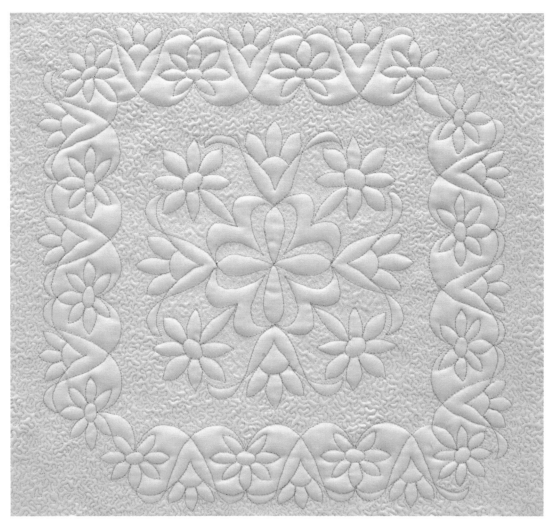

BONNY BLOOMS
Fabric: Cotton   **Batt:** Wool   **Thread:** Cotton (design), Silk (background)
Patterns: page 42 (border), page 43 (block)

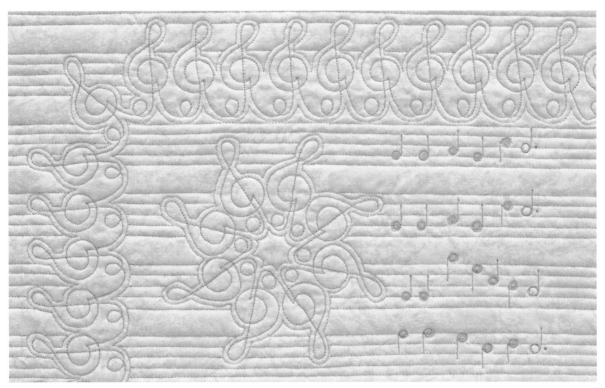

ONE-LINE SAMBA

Fabric: Cotton   **Batt:** Bamboo   **Thread:** Rayon (design), Silk (background)

Pattern: page 48

DANCING HEARTS

Fabric: Cotton   **Batt:** Bamboo   **Thread:** Rayon (design), Silk (background)

Pattern: page 89

OLD OAK

Fabric: Cotton

Batt: Bamboo

Thread: Polyester (design), Silk (background)

Pattern: page 61

RODEO

Fabric: Cotton denim

Batt: 80/20 Cotton/Polyester

Thread: Cotton

Pattern: page 60

GARDEN CHAIN

Fabric: Cotton   **Batt:** Wool

Thread: Polyester (design), Silk (background)

Pattern: page 84

SIMPLY SWIRLS

Fabric: Cotton

Batt: Wool

Thread: Rayon (design), Cotton (background)

Pattern: page 53

DO-SI-DO
Fabric: Cotton   **Batt:** 80/20 Cotton/Polyester
Thread: Cotton,
Pattern: page 44

VENETIAN WAVES
Fabric: Cotton
Batt: Wool
Thread: Cotton (design), Silk (background)
Pattern: page 41

GROUND COVER
Fabric: Cotton   **Batt:** 50/50 Cotton/silk
Thread: Cotton (design), Silk (background)
Pattern: page 40

APHRODITE
Fabric: Cotton   **Batt:** 90/10 Silk/cotton
Thread: Rayon (design), Silk (background)
Pattern: page 51

AUTUMN DANCE
Fabric: Cotton   **Batt:** Wool
Thread: Rayon (design),
Silk (background)
Pattern: page 81

LOVELY LILY
Fabric: 60/40 Cotton/silk   **Batt:** Silk
Thread: Rayon (design), Silk (background)
Pattern: page 46

DAHLIA DANDY
Fabric: Cotton batiste   **Batt:** Polyester
Thread: Polyester (design), Silk (background)
Pattern: page 46

Leaf Vein Stitching Options

Option 1: Stitch right next to one side of the line going in and right next to the other side of the vein going back toward the base of the leaf.

Option 2: Stitch directly on the vein line, and stitch directly on top of your stitches when going back to the base of the leaf.

Autumn Dance Stitching Diagrams

Begin stitching anywhere; you will finish where you began. As you come to the base of each leaf, stitch the vein of the leaf first, and then the outline of the leaf. Use the swirl to get to the next leaf.

For a simpler design, you can eliminate the leaf veins.

Pattern: *7″ × 7″* • **Stitched example:** page 68

See the matching border and overall stitching diagram on page 83.

Button
(center circle detail)

To the ribbon on the right side

End here.

To the ribbon on the left side

To the lower
flower stems

Leaf detail

Flower detail

Border: 2½″ • **Stitched example:** page 68

See the matching block on page 82.

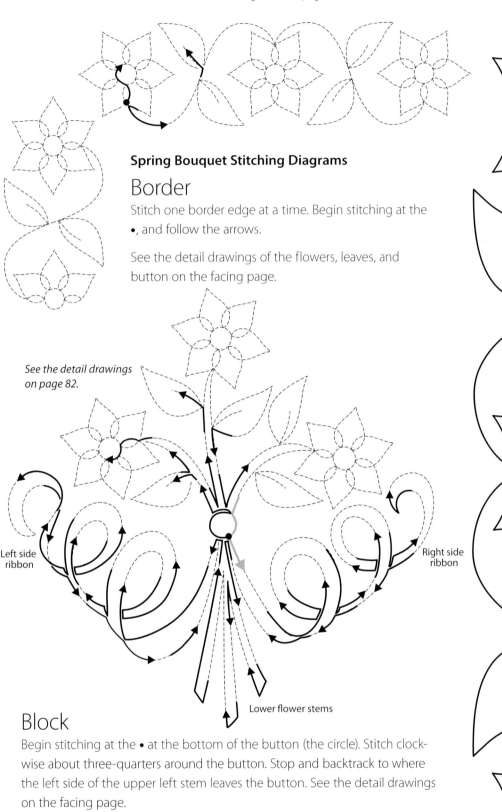

Spring Bouquet Stitching Diagrams

Border

Stitch one border edge at a time. Begin stitching at the •, and follow the arrows.

See the detail drawings of the flowers, leaves, and button on the facing page.

See the detail drawings on page 82.

Left side ribbon

Right side ribbon

Lower flower stems

Block

Begin stitching at the • at the bottom of the button (the circle). Stitch clockwise about three-quarters around the button. Stop and backtrack to where the left side of the upper left stem leaves the button. See the detail drawings on the facing page.

Follow the arrows up the stem, and stitch all the leaves, flowers, and stems. Then stitch the right side of the button back to the •. Now follow the arrows to stitch the ribbon on the right.

To achieve the twisted look on the ribbon, there are a few places you will backtrack. After stitching the ribbon on the right side, follow the arrows to stitch the lower flower stems, and then stitch the ribbon on the left side.

Continuous-Line Patterns

Garden Chain Stitching Diagrams

Begin stitching at the •, and stitch down one side of the leaf. Follow the gray arrows to stitch one side of the center chain. As you stitch the second side of that chain, at each corner, follow the arrows for stitching the leaves and the flower. Then finish another section of chain to reach the next corner with leaves and flowers.

When you arrive back at the •, follow the arrows to stitch twice around the outer chain to complete the chain.

Flower and leaf detail

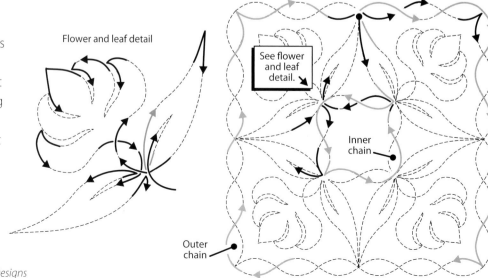

See flower and leaf detail.

Inner chain

Outer chain

Pattern: *7˝ × 7˝* • **Stitched example:** page 74

See a compatible border (Summer Leaves) on page 38.

Songbird Tree Stitching Diagrams

You may want to embroider (by hand or machine) the eyes before you quilt. Begin stitching at the •, and follow the arrows. For the bird and leaf details, see the detail drawings. Finish stitching where you began.

Bird detail

Leaf detail

See the matching block on page 87.

When you turn the motifs 90° to meet at the corners, trim this line here to create a corner, as shown.

Supreme Courting Border Stitching Diagram

Follow the arrows carefully. Begin stitching at •. If you arrange the corner as shown, you can stitch all the way around your project with one continuous line.

Repeat

Pattern: *7″ × 7″* • **Stitched example:** page 70

See the matching border on page 86.

Supreme Courting Stitching Diagram
Stitch the scalloped inner line first. Then begin stitching at the •, and stitch in one continuous line until you arrive back at the •.

Add a little bit of length here for a connecting corner.

End here.

Delicious Stitching Diagrams

Block

Begin stitching at the •, and stitch toward the handle. Follow the arrows to stitch the apple, and complete the handle and the basket. Hmmm … delicious!

Border

For a border that is continuous, add a little length to the line that connects the apples at the corners. Begin stitching anywhere, and follow the arrows.

As shown in this diagram, this configuration of the border apples and basket, in the size printed here, fits nicely in a 10″ block.

Add line extensions here for going around a corner.

Dancing Hearts Stitching Diagrams

Border

Begin stitching anywhere.
Follow the arrows.

Block

Hear the heartbeat?
Follow the arrows.

Ribbon Galaxy Stitching Diagram

This design can be a little challenging because of the parallel arcs. Begin stitching at the •, and follow the arrows up to the first ribbon. Use the center star shape to travel from ribbon to ribbon, and you will finish where you began. It is interesting to watch this design develop.

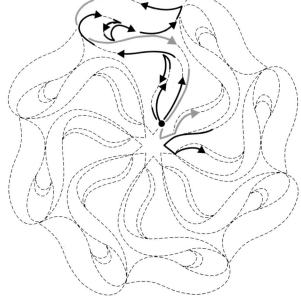

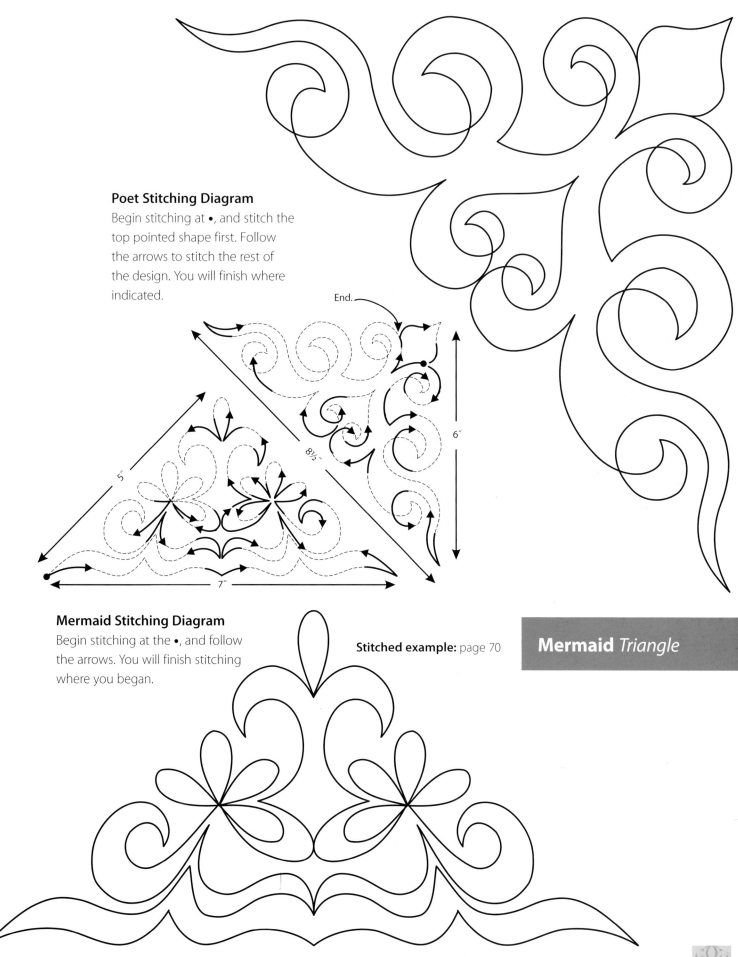

Poet Stitching Diagram

Begin stitching at •, and stitch the top pointed shape first. Follow the arrows to stitch the rest of the design. You will finish where indicated.

Mermaid Stitching Diagram

Begin stitching at the •, and follow the arrows. You will finish stitching where you began.

Splish Splash Stitching Diagrams

Splish Splash is stitched with 2 lines. The inner line, shown on its own at left, is a nice, simple design on its own.

With both lines, begin stitching anywhere. Follow the arrows when stitching the inner line. The outer wave line is just 1 line.

Say It with Flowers Stitching Diagram

Begin stitching at the •, and stitch the heart first. The arrows show you how to stitch the leaves and flowers. You will finish where you began.

Feathered Friend Stitching Diagrams

To avoid confusing the lines, there are occasional changes in the arrows (black to gray). When part of a directional line is dashed, backstitch over previous stitches. In the places where you backstitch, slow down. Do not watch the needle; look at the stitches on which you are backstitching.

1. Stitch the body line first, beginning at the •, and stitch the spine of the body.

2. Follow the face detail. Note the small amount of backstitching required around the beak. When you arrive at the ★, see the corresponding ★ on feather line.

3. Follow the feather line to complete the design.

When stitching the dividing line between the upper and lower beak, be sure to stitch all the way to the point of the beak before turning back.

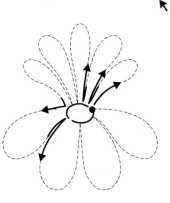

Fresh Flower Stitching Diagram

Begin at the •. Stitch the entire center oval, and then stitch the petals as shown.

Bird pattern: 8½″ × 6½″ • Flower pattern: 2½″ × 2½″
Stitched examples: page 69 • Stitching diagrams: page 94

Sunshine Chorus Stitching Diagram

Begin stitching at the •, and stitch toward the middle flower. Stitch the center of the flower before stitching the petals. When you are finished with the center flower, finish that corner leaf, and arrive back at the •. Travel on the *inner line* and stitch each corner leaf motif.

When you have finished the inner line and corner leaves, you will arrive back at the •. Follow the arrows to travel on the *outer line,* which will lead you to stitch side and corner flowers. Follow the arrows, and finish at the •.

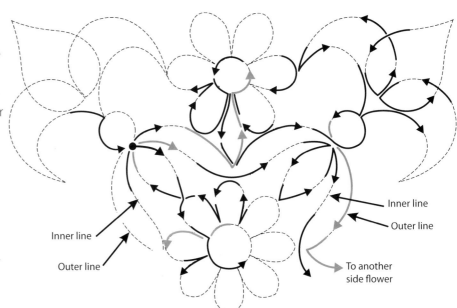

Inner line

Outer line

Inner line

Outer line

To another side flower

SUNSHINE CHORUS
Fabric: Cotton **Batt:** Wool **Thread:** Cotton
Pattern: page 96

MOLLY'S TULIPS
Fabric: Cotton   **Batt:** Wool   **Thread:** Polyester (design), Cotton (background)
Pattern: page 32

COLORADO SPRINGTIME
Fabric: Polyester blend   **Batt:** Wool
Thread: Polyester (design), Silk (background)
Pattern: page 28

MADRIGAL
Fabric: Cotton   **Batt:** 80/20 Cotton/polyester blend
Thread: Polyester (design), Cotton (background)
Pattern: page 18

NOSEGAY
Fabric: Cotton   **Batt:** Wool   **Thread:** Cotton
Pattern: page 25

SPLISH SPLASH
Fabric: Cotton   **Batt:** 50/50 Cotton/silk blend
Thread: Cotton
Pattern: page 92

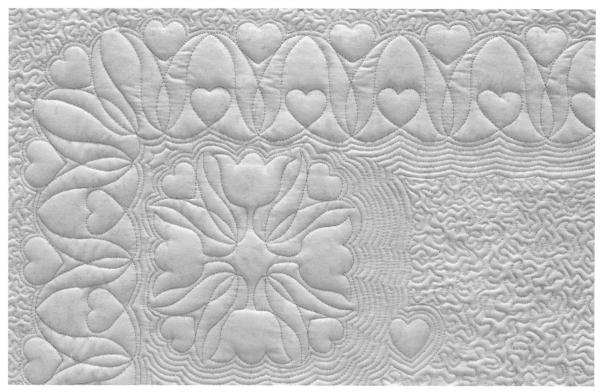

DUTCH ROMANCE
Fabric: Cotton   **Batt:** Wool   **Thread:** Rayon (design), Cotton (background)
Pattern: page 19

SUNNY FLOWERS
Fabric: Cotton   **Batt:** 80/20 Cotton/polyester   **Thread:** Cotton
Pattern: page 20

SIMPLE MELODY
Fabric: Cotton   **Batt:** Wool
Thread: Rayon (design), Cotton (background)   **Pattern:** page 33

CLOSE HARMONY
Pattern: page 39

SUMMER LEAVES
Pattern: page 38

Background Stitches

Backgrounds are stitched in areas directly next to quilting designs you want to showcase. They give the impression of receding behind a motif, much as a sky is in the background of a landscape painting. Some quilters call these stitches "fills."

These four pages contain a few ideas about background quilting in general.

A Good Background

Good background stitching adds texture and richness to your quilt without detracting from the featured quilting design. This texture is created by the quilting lines being closer to each other than the lines in the main quilting design.

Background quilting can appear a bit darker than the quilted design, even when the same thread is used for the design and the background. This is because lines of stitching create ditches when the quilt layers are compressed. The ditches create shadows. Background quilting has many lines of stitches close to each other, so more shadows are created. This slightly darker, textural effect is a lovely design element.

What Works

When deciding how close to stitch the lines of quilting in your background, consider how large or complex the quilted designs are. Make your background quilting dense enough so your quilting design will stand out.

The goal is not to make these lines of background stitches as close to each other as possible, but to space them so they best show off your quilted designs. Very small motifs need closer background stitching to increase the contrast. Larger motifs do not need the same density.

It often helps to experiment on a small sample piece with a portion of the quilting design to see how tightly you want to stitch the background. If your stitches are too widely spaced for the design, you miss an opportunity to accent the design.

Density makes a difference.

Threads

The effect that the background has on the design is also influenced by the threads you use. I have the most fun and success using thin threads such as 100-weight silk, 50–60-weight cotton, and 60-weight polyester when stitching backgrounds. These threads are easy to manipulate while free-motion quilting, and their lighter weight contrasts nicely with the slightly heavier threads that are often used when stitching the designs.

Techniques

Pencil and Paper

A great way to develop confidence with an unfamiliar background stitch is to use pencil and paper. Practice drawing the lines of stitching.

To become familiar with a background idea that is new to me, I fill sheets of paper with pencil drawings. I concentrate on these drawings just as though I were quilting at my sewing machine. Sometimes I use a fine-point felt tip pen when I draw because it cannot be erased. That teaches me to pay close attention, trains my concentration for sewing, and gives me confidence

Backgrounds with a Presser Foot

A presser foot with feed teeth up is used to quilt most long, straight lines or very gentle, simple curves. With a little practice, you can quilt short straight lines with free-motion techniques.

A grid marked on your quilt top helps when you want to stitch straight lines or when straight lines are used as a guide for other stitching. Mark the lines before the quilt sandwich is made, if you know ahead you will need them, or as soon as you realize that guidelines would be useful. It is difficult to mark good straight lines on the quilt top after it is sandwiched and partially quilted. This is especially true if a fluffy batt is used.

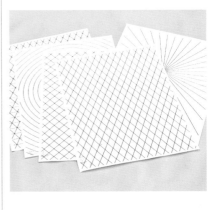

To aid in marking lines, I have drawn several types of grids on paper. These grids have lines with a variety of spacings, angles, concentric circles, and so on. They are very handy for tracing and marking.

Echo Quilting

A simple description of echo quilting is a line of stitching surrounding a quilting design. The distance of the echo from the design is determined by personal taste and creative decisions. This line can be repeated as often as you like, keeping in mind that each line loses a little definition as you add "echoes."

One round of echo quilting often closes gaps that might be present on the edges of the main quilting motif. This is useful when you want to add background stitching to the outside of the design but not to the interior of the design.

Echo quilting was very helpful to me while stitching the quilted examples in this book.

Common Background Stitches

The more you use background stitching, the faster you will develop your own style. Like all good quilting, backgrounds are as individual as personal signatures.

Ever-Useful Stippling

Stippling is to background quilting like the letter "e" is to our written language. We see it used everywhere, and we might get tired of needing it, but it sure comes in handy. Stippling travels from one area to another easily, can be stitched in a wide variety of densities, can fill any shaped space, and it complements and works well with other background stitches. I use stippling techniques frequently, in a variety of ways.

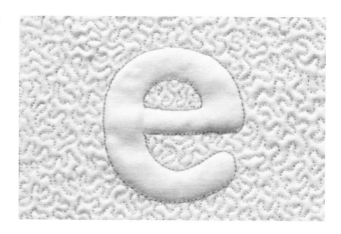

When quilting a background, we want to prevent pleats and puckers and avoid stitching ourselves into a corner. If these are difficulties you encounter when stippling, some of the following ideas might help. I call this Subdivide and Escape.

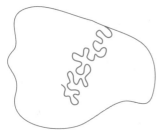

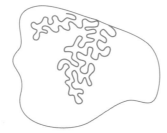

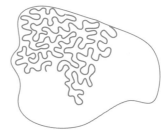

1. Begin at an edge, and stitch a bouncy, wiggly line into the middle of the area you want to stipple, but do not stitch to the edge on the other side. By not stitching all the way to the other side, you have left an "escape" route.

2. Loosely follow the first line back to almost where you began. Now you have made a "subdivision." This helps to prevent pleats and puckers by distributing fabric and batting evenly.

Make another, smaller subdivision.

3. To fill in a subdivision, make your bouncy lines next to your most recent (newest) stitches. To avoid stitching yourself into a corner, whenever you are faced with a decision as to where to go next, always stay next to your most recent stitches.

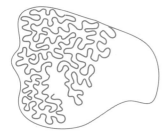

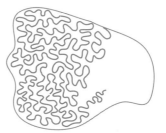

4. Use your escape routes to travel from one subdivision to another. Fill each subdivision, remembering to enter the subdivision next to your most recent stitches.

5. After one side of your main area is stitched, use the escape route you initially created to get to the other side. Continue to make subdivisions and leave escape routes.

Olé

This Olé background effect is seen in April Delight (page 75) and Madrigal (page 99).

If you haven't stitched this type of design, consider drawing it on paper to get the feel of it.

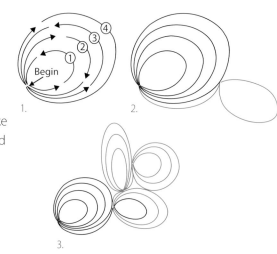

1. Make an initial loop about ⅜″–½″. (You will soon decide whether you like a larger or smaller size for your quilting.) Reverse stitching direction, and add 2 or 3 larger loops around the first loop.

2. To add another set of loops and change direction, make an arc (partial loop) to touch the last loop made, at the place where you want to begin another set of loops. Add another small loop (2).

3. Stitch larger loops around the new small loop (3). Continue to make new sets of loops. Don't concern yourself about having all the starter loops the exact same size. The slight variety is nice.

Pancakes

Pancakes can be seen in Night Light (page 76) and Garden Chain (page 78).

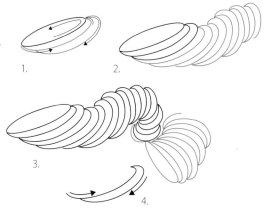

1. Stitch a narrow oval (black line). Next, stitch an arc (partial oval) back to the top of that first oval. Reverse direction and stitch another arc, but don't go all the way to the base of the first oval (blue line).

2. Stack as many pancakes as you like. The direction of your "stack" and the size of your pancakes depend on where you touch the last arc you made (2).

3. When you want to start another stack, stop midway on an arc and change direction with a new oval (3). Continue stacking.

Except for the top pancake, individual pancake lines will be similar to this.

Background Bling

Consider adding a little "bling" to some of your backgrounds. It doesn't have to be much to add a smile or interest—a heart here, a star there. …

Use the same thread as your background quilting to add a subtle touch, or change thread for a bit more attention.

See backgrounds of Catnap (page 72), Dancing Hearts (page 77), and Sunshine Chorus (page 97).

DEBRA WAGNER— THE OHIO BRIDES QUILT

In the 1990s, at what is now the National Quilt Museum in Paducah, Kentucky, I saw a quilt named *Ohio Brides Quilt,* made by Debra Wagner of Minnesota. My heart almost stopped—the quilt was so lovely. The machine-quilted motifs were beautifully accented. I have not seen the actual quilt since that night at the museum. Although the quilt still frequently roams around in my head, I cannot tell you anything about the background stitching. This must be because the background stitches so perfectly complemented the rest of the quilting. With her sublime creativity and exquisite workmanship, Debra raised the bar for many of us.

Marking (or Not)

Mark your quilt for quilting before you make the quilt sandwich.

For most of my marking, I use the blue, water-soluble, rinse-out pens. I have never had a problem with the pigment staying in or staining a quilt. I am cautious not to iron over the marks, leave them in a quilt once I have finished quilting it, or leave a marked piece in the trunk of my car on a hot day. I buy several of these pens at a time and rotate them while I am marking designs. For very dark fabrics, I use a white pencil that rinses out.

Before I begin marking my quilt tops, I test the marking tools on all of the fabrics I'm using to make sure that the marks will come out of each fabric.

If the fabric you want to mark is light colored, you can usually place the pattern underneath the fabric and see through the fabric. If the fabric is dark enough that you can't see through it, use a simple plastic lightbox with an inexpensive under-the-counter kitchen lamp underneath it.

When using a lightbox, make sure that the pattern is printed only on one side. Otherwise it will be difficult to see the pattern lines clearly.

If you don't want to put any marks on your fabric:

1. Trace the design on one sheet of inexpensive school tracing paper. (Supermarkets often have this in the school supply aisle.) Put this marked sheet on top of a stack with up to nine other sheets of the tracing paper, or fewer if you only need a few. Pin or staple the pages together.

2. Take the thread out of the sewing machine, and put an old, dull, large needle in the machine. Follow the design lines on the top sheet of marked paper, and stitch through all of the sheets of paper. This will perforate them all.

3. Place a sheet of this perforated tracing on top of the quilt sandwich, and pin it to hold in place.

4. Stitch on the perforated lines. The design will be easy to see, and the predrilled little holes make it easy to stitch through and to remove the paper.

Enlarging and Reducing Patterns

If you don't have a copier that enlarges/reduces, you can go to a local copy shop. If needed, a limited copyright release is on page 2 of this book.

Because enlarging a pattern can distort the pattern a tiny amount, the patterns in this book were printed as large as space and page design would allow. This makes enlarging easier. Reducing is rarely a problem with copiers.

Chart 1 is for converting fractions to decimals. Most patterns (including the patterns in this book) provide measurements in fractions. If you measure a pattern with a ruler, anything less than an inch will be a fraction. However, your handy-dandy little calculator thinks in decimals, so you must convert the fractions to decimals.

CHART 1: Converting fractions to decimals

⅛″	=	.125″	⅝″	=	.625″
¼″	=	.25″	¾″	=	.75″
⅜″	=	.375″	⅞″	=	.875″
½″	=	.5″	1″	=	1.0″

The formulas at right show how to find the percentage of enlargement/reduction needed to get the desired pattern size.

Divide the size you want by the size you *have*.

Example 1: Enlarging a design

You want a 9½″ design. You have a 7¼″ design.

1. Enter 9.5 into your calculator.

2. Press the divide sign (/ or ÷) and enter 7.25.

3. Press the equal sign (=).

The answer is 1.31, which means to set the copier at 131% and copy your original. (In this particular case, you would have to use copy paper larger than letter size or copy the design on two sheets of paper.)

Example 2: Reducing a design

You want a 4¼″ design. You have a 6½″ design.

1. Enter 4.25 into your calculator.

2. Press the divide sign (/ or ÷) and enter 6.5.

3. Press the equal sign (=).

The answer is .65, which means to set the copier at 65% and copy your pattern.

CHART 2: Common percentages for enlarging and reducing patterns in this book

Enlargement and reduction sizes are percentages; reduction sizes are shaded. Percentages of more than 200% or less than 50% are not listed.

Patterns in this book	You **want** this size																						
	2″	2½″	3″	3½″	4″	4½″	5″	5½″	6″	6½″	7″	7½″	8″	8½″	9″	9½″	10″	10½″	11″	11½″	12″	12½″
2″	0		150	175	200																	
2¼″	88	111	133	156	177	200																
2½″	80	0	120	140	160	180	200															
3″	66	83	0	117	133	150	166	183	200													
3½″	57	71	86	0	114	129	143	157	171	186	200											
4″	50	62	75	88	0	112	125	138	150	162	175	187	200									
4½″		55	66	77	89	0	111	122	133	144	155	167	177									
5″		50	60	70	80	90	0	110	120	130	140	150	160	170	180	190	200					
5¼″			57	66	76	86	95	104	114	124	133	143	152	162	171	181	190	200				
5½″			55	64	73	82	91	0	109	118	127	136	145	155	164	173	182	191	200			
6″			50	58	67	75	83	91	0	108	117	125	133	142	150	158	167	175	183	192	200	
6½″				54	62	69	77	85	92	0	108	115	123	131	138	146	154	162	169	177	184	192
7″				50	57	64	71	78	86	93	0	107	114	121	129	136	143	150	157	164	171	179
7½″					53	60	66	73	80	87	93	0	106	113	120	127	133	140	147	153	160	167
8½″						53	59	65	70	76	82	88	94	0	106	112	118	123	129	135	141	147

Easy-Find Design Index

Aphrodite
Pattern 51   Stitched example 79

April Delight
Pattern 24   Stitched example 75

April Delight Border
Pattern 24   Stitched example 75

Autumn Dance
Pattern 81   Stitched example 80

Aztec
Pattern 59   Stitched example 71

Aztec Borders
Pattern 58   Stitched example 71

Bonny Blooms
Pattern 43   Stitched example 76

Bonny Blooms Border
Pattern 42   Stitched example 76

Butterfly Beauties
Pattern 37   Stitched example 67

Butterfly Beauties Border
Pattern 36   Stitched example 67

Camelot
Pattern 17   Stitched example 16

Candy Box
Pattern 45   Stitched example 75

Catnap
Pattern 34   Stitched example 72

Close Harmony
Pattern 39   Stitched example 101

Colorado Springtime
Pattern 28   Stitched example 99

Crescent Charm
Pattern 57   Stitched example 71

Dahlia Dandy
Pattern 46   Stitched example 80

Daisy Ballet
Pattern 26   Stitched example 73

Daisy Ballet Border
Pattern 27   Stitched example 73

Dancing Hearts
Pattern 89   Stitched example 77

Dancing Hearts Border
Pattern 89   Stitched example 77

Deco Delight
Pattern 56   Stitched example 71

Delicious
Pattern 88   Stitched example 75

Delicious Border
Pattern 88   Stitched example 75

Doily
Pattern 47   Stitched example 69

Do-Si-Do
Pattern 44   Stitched example 79

Dutch Romance
Pattern 19   Stitched example 100

Dutch Romance Border
Pattern 19   Stitched example 100

Elegance
Pattern 55   Stitched example 68

Elegance Border
Pattern 55   Stitched example 68

Feathered Friend
Pattern 95   Stitched example 69

Floral Galaxy
Pattern 21   Stitched example 66

Floral Galaxy Border
Pattern 22   Stitched example 66

Formal Dinner
Pattern 31   Stitched example 72

Formal Dinner Border
Pattern 30   Stitched example 72

Foxy Feline
Pattern 35   Stitched example 72

Fresh Flower
Pattern 95   Stitched example 69

Friendship
Pattern 50   Stitched example 74

Garden Chain
Pattern 84   Stitched example 78

Ground Cover
Pattern 40   Stitched example 79

Lavender Blues
Pattern 23   Stitched example 66

Lavender Blues Border
Pattern 22   Stitched example 66

Little Feathered Nest
Pattern 47   Stitched example 69

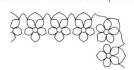

Lovely Lily
Pattern 46   Stitched example 80

Madrigal
Pattern 18   Stitched example 99

Mermaid Triangle
Pattern 91   Stitched example 70

Merry Mouse
Pattern 35   Stitched example 72

Molly's Tulips
Pattern 32   Stitched example 98

Night Light Border
Pattern 52   Stitched example 76

Nosegay
Pattern 25   Stitched example 99

Old Oak
Pattern 61   Stitched example 78

Index continued →

One-Line Samba
Pattern 48 Stitched example 77

One-Line Samba Border
Pattern 48 Stitched example 77

Only Hearts
Pattern 63 Stitched example 73

Only Hearts Border
Pattern 62 Stitched example 73

Only Hearts Triangle
Pattern 62 Stitched example 73

Poet Triangle
Pattern 91 Stitched example 70

Ribbon Galaxy
Pattern 90 Stitched example 74

Rodeo
Pattern 60 Stitched example 78

Say It with Flowers
Pattern 93 Stitched example 67

Simple Melody
Pattern 33 Stitched example 101

Simply Swirls
Pattern 53 Stitched example 78

Sleepy Time
Pattern 34 Stitched example 72

Songbird Tree
Pattern 85 Stitched example 74

Splendid Swan
Pattern 64 Stitched example 65

Splish Splash
Pattern 92 Stitched example 99

Spring Basket
Pattern 54 Stitched example 75

Spring Bouquet
Pattern 82 Stitched example 68

Spring Bouquet Border
Pattern 83 Stitched example 68

Starshine
Pattern 29 Stitched example 67

Summer Leaves
Pattern 38 Stitched example 101

Sunny Flowers
Pattern 20 Stitched example 100

Sunny Flowers Border
Pattern 20 Stitched example 100

Sunshine Chorus
Pattern 96 Stitched example 97

Supreme Courting
Pattern 87 Stitched example 70

Supreme Courting Border
Pattern 86 Stitched example 70

Surf's Up Border
Pattern 52 Stitched example 65

Sweet Adeline
Pattern 49 Stitched example 74

Venetian Waves
Pattern 41 Stitched example 79

About the Author

Hari Walner applies her years of experience as an illustrator and designer to her work as a designer in the quilt world. She received fine art and illustration training at the Colorado Institute of Art in Denver and The American Academy of Art in Chicago.

For many years she taught painting and drawing in her studio in Silver Spring, Maryland, and now uses those skills when teaching machine quilting in classes and workshops. In 2006 she was named Teacher of the Year by *The Professional Quilter* magazine.

This is the third book Hari has written for C&T Publishing. Her earlier books, *Trapunto by Machine* and *Exploring Machine Trapunto,* were based on a machine trapunto technique she developed in the 1990s.

The majority of her teaching is in the United States, occasionally in the beautiful studio that Gordon Snow, her partner/husband, built for her in 2006. She and Gordon share three adult children, four grandchildren, and their dog Piper. Hari lives near Loveland, Colorado.

Also by Hari Walner:

Resources

The products listed here are products I used in this book.

These businesses offer many more fine products.

Silk, wool, cotton, and poly batting

Hobbs Bonded Fibers
200 South Commerce Drive
Waco, TX 76710
www.hobbsbondedfibers.com

Cotton, wool, poly, and green batting

Quilter's Dream Batting
589 Central Drive
Virginia Beach, VA 23454
www.quiltersdreambatting.com

Hand-dyed batik fabric

Sew Batik
879 Main Street West
Mayville, ND 58257
www.sewbatik.com

**40-wt. rayon thread;
12- and 30-wt. cotton thread**

Sulky of America
980 Cobb Place Blvd., Suite 130
Kennesaw, GA 30144
www.sulky.com

**60-wt. polyester thread;
40-wt. cotton thread**

Superior Threads
87 East 2580 South
St. George, UT 84790
www.superiorthreads.com

Designer 1 Sewing Machine

Husqvarna Viking
P.O. Box 7017
LaVergne, TN 37086
www.husqvarnaviking.com

100-wt. silk thread

YLI Corporation
1435 Dave Lyle Blvd. #16C
Rock Hill, SC 29730
www.ylicorp.com

Great Titles *from* C&T PUBLISHING

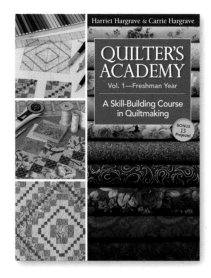

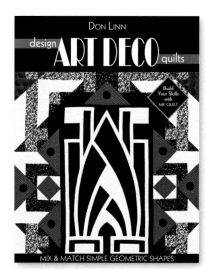

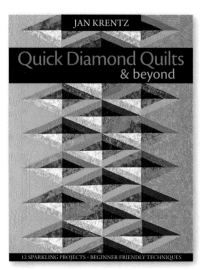

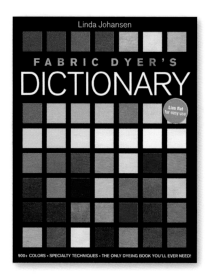

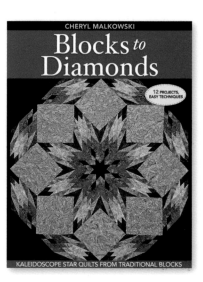

Available at your local retailer or **www.ctpub.com** *or* **800-284-1114**

For a list of other fine books from C&T Publishing, visit our website
to view our catalog online

C&T PUBLISHING, INC.

P.O. Box 1456
Lafayette, CA 94549
800-284-1114

Email: ctinfo@ctpub.com
Website: www.ctpub.com

C&T Publishing's professional photography services are now available to
the public. Visit us at www.ctmediaservices.com.

Tips and Techniques can be found at www.ctpub.com > Consumer
Resources > Quiltmaking Basics: Tips & Techniques for Quiltmaking & More

For quilting supplies:

COTTON PATCH

1025 Brown Ave.
Lafayette, CA 94549
Store: 925-284-1177
Mail order: 925-283-7883

Email: CottonPa@aol.com
Website: www.quiltusa.com

Note: Fabrics used in the quilts shown may not be currently
available, as fabric manufacturers keep most fabrics in print for
only a short time.